Changing Shape:
New and Selected Poems

EDWARD LUCIE-SMITH was born in 1933 in Kingston, Jamaica. He was educated at King's School, Canterbury and Merton College, Oxford, where he read History. After service as an Education Officer in the RAF, he worked in advertising for ten years before becoming a freelance author. He is a prolific and widely published writer on art. Several of his books, including *Movements in Art since 1945*, *Visual Arts of the Twentieth Century*, *A Dictionary of Art Terms* and *Art Today* are used as standard texts throughout the world. He is a poet and anthologist, and a photographer whose work is represented in the National Portrait Gallery in London.

Also by Edward Lucie-Smith

A Tropical Childhood and other poems
Confessions and Histories
Towards Silence
The Well-Wishers

EDWARD LUCIE-SMITH

Changing Shape

New and Selected Poems

CARCANET

for Drue Heinz,
patron of poetry

This edition first published in Great Britain in 2002 by
Carcanet Press Limited
4th Floor, Conavon Court
12–16 Blackfriars Street
Manchester M3 5BQ

A CIP catalogue record for this book
is available from the British Library

ISBN 1 85754 549 4

The publisher acknowledges financial assistance
from the Arts Council of England.

Set in Monotype Garamond by XL Publishing Services, Tiverton
Printed and bound in England by SRP Ltd, Exeter

Contents

from *A Tropical Childhood and other poems* (1962)

A Tropical Childhood	3
At the Roman Baths, Bath	3
June Bug	4
Kifissia	5
Meeting Myself	6
On Looking at Stubbs's *Anatomy of the Horse*	6
Pelicans	7
Rabbit Cry	8
Street Market Singer	8
Take Count Then, Sir…	9
The Lesson	10
The Portrait	10
The Temptation of St Antony	11
Wishes	12

from *Confessions and Histories* (1964)

A Caged Beast	15
A Stone	15
Distances	16
Epiclesis	17
Imperialists in Retirement	19
Pietà	20
The Barbarian Invasions	20
The Link	21
The Naming	21
The Wise Child	22
To Be Justified	22
Vanitas	23

from *Towards Silence* (1968)

Adam and Tristan	27
Alteration	27
Christmas Snowfall	28

Fragment of a 'Tristan' – I   29
Fragment of a 'Tristan' – II   30
Gallipoli: Fifty Years After   31
Genesis   33
Gran Tierra, Cuba   34
'Heureux Qui, Comme Ulysse…'   35
Looking at a Drawing   36
'Oh To Be That Round O!'   36
Silence   37
Spider Man   37
Tainted Fruit   38
Teeth and Bones   38
The Bureaucrat   39
The Drowning Dream   39
The Researcher   40
Three Songs for Surrealists   40
Your Own Place   43

from *The Well-Wishers* (1974)

An Epitaph   47
Asleep   48
At Forty   48
Bamboo Shoots   49
Beds   49
Descending   50
Lovers   50
North-West Passage   54
On Blackness   55
On Light   55
Postcard   56
Snow Poem   56
The Dawn Ray   57
The Interview   57
The Photograph   58
The Son   59
The Well-Wishers   59
Touching   60
Translated to Translator   61
Your Grandmother's Mark   62

Uncollected Poems (1974–1995)

A Former Lover 65
A Happy Snap 66
Azaleas 66
'Blackbirds are Eating…' 67
Clothing 67
Crystal Ball 68
Dancing 68
Eclipse 69
Five Morsels in the Form of Pears 69
Gone 71
Holbein's *Lady With a Squirrel* 72
In California 72
In Secret 73
Inscriptions 73
'It's the Season for Broken Hearts' 78
Klee's Angels 79
Night Music 82
Pan and Echo 82
Poems for Clocks 84
'Sleepily Murmuring…' 86
Sparrows 87
The Lagoon 87
The Outcry 88
The Welcome 88
Things of this World 89
Undressing 90
Velasquez's *An Old Woman Cooking Eggs* 90
Welsh Weather 91

Uncollected Poems (1995–2001)

A Letter Home 95
A Little Ode 96
Affair 96
Cafard 97
Changing Shape 98
'Here for a Little While' 98
In Helsinki 99
In the Henhouse 99
In Two Words 100
Invitation to the Dance 100

Kosovo, 1999 – 1   101
Kosovo, 1999 – 2   102
Left-Handed   103
Leviathan   104
'Lost Roads…'   104
Minotaur   105
My Mother   105
Why is There no Female Michelangelo?   106
Obituaries   107
Oh God, Oh God   108
Poetry   108
Poetry Reading   109
Rain in Buenos Aires   110
Riding the Drum   111
Russian Elegy – 1   112
Russian Elegy – 2   113
The Great Poet   113
The Stone Ship   114
Words – 1   115
Words – 2   115

Afterword   117

from
A Tropical Childhood and other poems
(1962)

A Tropical Childhood

(during World War II)

In the hot noons I heard the fusillade
As soldiers on the range learned how to kill,
Used my toy microscope, whose lens arrayed
The twenty rainbows in a parrot's quill.

Or once, while I was swimming in the bay,
The guns upon the other, seaward shore
Began a practice shoot; the angry spray
Fountained above the point at every roar.

Then I, in the calm water, dived to chase
Pennies my father threw me, searched the sand
For the brown discs a yard beneath my face,
And never tried to see beyond my hand.

That was the time when a dead grasshopper,
Devoured by ants before my captive eye,
Made the sun dark, yet distant battles were
Names in a dream, outside geography.

At the Roman Baths, Bath

Between trains, on this day of snow,
I kill an hour here. The old man
Who swabs the pavement makes us two –
I'm solitary, not alone.
In the bleak water goldfish swallow
As if they gulped the snowflakes down.
What do I feel? I wish I knew –
Today thoughts swim, but feelings drown.

I see the snow twist back from steam
Above one fool; this other lies
Dragging the willing whiteness home,
Coldness to coldness. Back I gaze
At Sul-Minerva, chipped and grim –
The carving stares through centuries,
Celtic but Roman, *her* but *him*,
Reason's image with mad eyes.

The eyes are stone, but yet they weep –
Slow drops of water form and fall
(Steam mixed with snow in every drop).
I catch one running down the wall
And taste it from my fingertip –
It shocks the tongue with salt and chill:
This sign of a god's ownership
Can make me feel uneasy still.

June Bug

Bug like a coffee-bean
Thrown on this tabletop
Beside my paper and pen,
You startle me with your rap.

You, on this hot June night
Which opens window and door,
Come like an intimate
From June of a former year.

Then I, a boy with a book,
In a room where a bare bulb glared,
Slept – and struggled awake;
Round me the June bugs whirred.

And, by the inkwell, one
Trundled, a frill of wing
Glinting like cellophane:
On the very lip he clung…

You're off? No reason to feel
That *you*, sir, stand on the brink
Of some disastrous fall
Into a pool of ink.

Kifissia

Eyes. Hands. Husks opening. Clothing ripped at, cast
Broadcast upon the dry floor of the wood.
It's almost dark. Night filters through the pines.
Glimmering beneath them, white as flour or dust,
Our forked flesh waits the moment when it joins –
Machine looks at machine, and need at need.

And somewhere a dog barking, a dog barking.

Somewhere, not far, a city. Nearer still,
Verandas of the rich. A gramophone
Whining. Gossip. Nearest is the other.
A car is changing gear to climb the hill.
We are at one in what we do together,
Yet each feels wholly separate while it's done.

And somewhere a dog barking, a dog barking.

First there came lust – a hurt called to a hurt –
And then the sweats and shivering of the sick.
Soon it is over – comes the time for shame.
So now we cannot look. Each turns apart,
Groping for clothes, for buttons, for a name.
We cast each other off, take selfhood back.

And somewhere a dog barking, a dog barking.

A scent of beeswax, dust; the empty rooms
Echo my footfalls; I am on the stair,
Have brushed my arm against the vase of roses,
When suddenly I see him standing there
Amid the petals shaken from the blooms,
Wearing my clothes. I see the look he chooses.

'You're trespassing,' it says. 'Who let you in?
You should have got no nearer than the gate –
How did you come so softly up the gravel?'
My outstretched fingers stub against the plate
Of the long grass, our touch barred by the thin
Clearness between; our nod is barely civil.

On Looking at Stubbs's Anatomy of the Horse

In Lincolnshire, a village full of tongues
Not tired by a year's wagging, and a man
Shut in a room where a wrecked carcass hangs,
His calm knife peeling putrid flesh from bone;
He whistles softly, as an ostler would;
The dead horse moves, as if it understood.

That night a yokel holds the taproom still
With tales new-hatched; he's peeped, and seen a mare
Stand there alive with naked rib and skull –
The creature neighed, and stamped upon the floor;
The warlock asked her questions, and she spoke;
He wrote her answers down in a huge book…

Two centuries gone, I have the folio here,
And turn the pages, find them pitiless.
These charts of sinew, vein and bone require
A glance more expert, more detached than this –
Fingering the margins, I think of the old
Sway-backed and broken nags the pictures killed.

Yet, standing in that room, I watch the knife;
Light dances on it as it maps a joint
Or scribes a muscle; I am blank and stiff,
The blade cuts so directly to my want;
I grope for anecdote, absurd detail,
Like any yokel with his pint of ale.

Pelicans

In deserts of the bay
The stylite pelicans
Watch the world pass away.

Each calmly meditates
Perched on a tarry balk,
Immovable awaits

Answer to solemn prayer
Until a shoal of fish
Glitters in the dull air.

Then the rewarded saint
Is roused, and taking wing,
With swerve and cunning feint

He stoops above the sea —
No shrill irreverent bird
Could show more cruelty.

Rabbit Cry

The season? Not yet spring. The place? Beside
A knot of sapling birches, under sky
Silver as birch-bark. Here were gaping wide
A warren's crumbling mouths to catch our feet.
We stooped; the nets were staked, the bag untied,
And into day's eye glared a blood-red eye –
The ferret trembled, with a sudden slide
Plunged white to darkness. Hearts resumed their beat.

Yet memory's fixed by what I did not see.
It was as if I heard the birches creak
Under a troubling gust, as if each tree
Now drew up from its roots those shreds of words
That in the windless day surrounded me.
It was the warren's mouths began to shriek –
I saw their breathless immobility
Ajar to the still sky stripped bare of birds.

Street Market Singer

Cracked cups, dulled lacquer, tarnished silver – things
            Fingered, caressed;
It's hands I see, and money changing hands
Beside the gutter where the old man sings
        At nobody's request;
The crowds are thick, but thinnest where he stands.

I pause to hear him, often heard before –
            Interrogate
His grey face and the phlegm-obstructed drone
In which he chants those words of the First War,
        And wonder why I wait
To seek a meaning if the meaning's gone.

My father fought that war and sang that song;
          If you went there
You'd hardly trace the ditches where he fought;
He bred me late – I never saw him young;
          No craftsman can repair
This singer like the lacquer box I bought.

Staring right through me as the crowds divide,
          He claims no debt;
No cap's upturned for coins, his hands hang down;
Now it is I who'd not be put aside,
          Who by one glance am set
In my own world and told it's all I own.

Take Count Then, Sir…

Take count then, sir, how small you have to be
Whose image I find sculptured in a stone
          Picked shining from the sea,
          Whose voice has the harsh tone
          Of a storm-shaken tree.

For you are what I am (how small you are!),
As I contain you, mould your fluid shape
          To fit the earthen jar
          And in my limits keep
          Your sum of near and far.

You are not God; although I tear apart
The natural wholeness to compose your form;
          Within my narrow art
          I only trap the storm
          But never the storm's heart.

You from your central calm accept my 'no':
You cannot snare me if I think you caught,
          Nor, wrestler, make your throw
          Until I have been taught
          To let your semblance go.

The Lesson

'Your father's gone,' my bald headmaster said.
His shiny dome and brown tobacco jar
Splintered at once in tears. It wasn't grief.
I cried for knowledge which was bitterer
Than any grief. For there and then I knew
That grief has uses – that a father dead
Could bind the bully's fist a week or two;
And then I cried for shame, then for relief.

I was a month past ten when I learned this;
I still remember how the noise was stilled
In school assembly when my grief came in.
Some goldfish in a bowl quietly sculled
Around their shining prison on its shelf.
They were indifferent. All the other eyes
Were turned towards me. Somewhere in myself
Pride, like a goldfish, flashed a sudden fin.

The Portrait

Ranked on their shelves your motley *lares* stand;
Your curtains shudder softly in the breeze
That comes with dawn; your shoulders and your hair
Gleam by the single lamp, as does the hand
I stretch to touch your nape laid on my knees,
And by that gesture bring us strangely near
In solitude, and weariness, despair.

I'm sad the hour should find us so allied
By such a bond – my truth in answering;
You asked me whom I'd loved as if the game
Was played in the same spirit on each side,
As if no word could cost us anything,
As if I had no thought but to be tame:
Then I was truthful, gave you your own name.

That is the work I will not have unsaid –
Muttering and sullen, now the gas-fire burns
Yet lower, yet more blue, and darkly stares
Down from the shadowy frame above my head
Your sixteenth-century man; indifferent, turns
A sensual gaze on our remote affairs
While something in us that indifference shares.

The Temptation of St Antony

He in the mirror of the air looks back
And frightening in the dusk of summer sees
The human-headed falcon on his track.

Easy the dusk of summer: not at ease
The encircling landscape or the quiet stream
Where a huge fish leaps through the doubled trees.

But, being a simple man, he calls it dream,
And as he hurries to the rectory gate
Will not allow that things are as they seem.

Within, a fire is burning on the grate,
His daughter knits. His sermon still to write,
He draws the curtains, says he will be late.

And while the church-clock measures out the night,
Prays God for blindness of his second sight.

Wishes

(for William, aged seven weeks)

I ought to wish you all that's moderate –
Just wits enough, and more, but not much more
Money than most, and even health in measure;
A man who's never sick is too cocksure.
It's my clear duty. Who gets any pleasure
From dutiful wishing? Let me wish you great
Troubles, great gifts; and crooked roads, not straight.

Not all that many wishes, you perceive,
But quite enough to make things difficult.
You think, perhaps, you've much to cry for now.
But when you cry you've hopes of some result –
Mother comes running if you keep the row
Loud enough long enough. But life can leave
You crying longer than you would believe.

from
Confessions and Histories
(1964)

A Caged Beast

This other world: we cannot look at it
Without a lie – the looking is a lie.
'Like us,' we say, to all their calmer motions.
'Like us.' to every evidence of wit.
The narrow pupil of the leopard's eye
Contains more flattery than we'll admit;
We gesture there, performing our devotions
Not to the supple back, the rapid paw,
But to ourselves. That little mirror is
All of the leopard we have patience for.

But why so eager to catch likenesses?
The caged beast thrusts his head against the bars.
Two unreflecting wounds, two gazing scars.

A Stone

Found where I had so often
Trodden. Soft limestone gnawed by
The jaws of water, the teeth
Of rain. White. Bone-white. A skull
Which was small enough to lie
Easily in my child's palm.
I remember that stone still –
Its hollow stare stopped my breath.

And yet, even then, I knew
Nothing would come of it, good
Or evil. It was mere stone,
Bone of the earth, not my bone
Come to haunt me here beside
The hedgebank. Picked up and tossed
Over the line of the hedge,
Startling a starling, rolling
Into a rut of the plough,
Its burial meant nothing,
And its resurrection
Nothing. Should the trumpet crow
Buried stone would lie there still.

But away on the dunghill,
As I threw the stone, I heard
A midday cockerel crow.

Distances

At a friend's house one autumn night,
A tale of loss and pain and fright;
    I hear his harsh voice still
    Which could not make me feel.

The shadow of a flapping blind,
Stains on the wall – these held the mind;
    I answered 'yes' and 'no',
    but soon got up to go.

Outside his door I saw the wind
Set scraps of paper whirling round –
    Nothing to make me stare,
    Those captives of the air.

Yet from the corner of an eye
I watched their flickering flight, the way
    They seemed, though so much dross,
    Inanimate and gross,

To skim and skip and play as if
They, not the nagging breeze, had life;
    I thought, 'An hour ago
    Would these have moved me so?'

For, strangely, in that quiet street
I heard my pulse's stumbling beat,
    Louder, less regular,
    Than passing footsteps were.

And, as I watched, one dusty scrap
Doubled a doorstep's stormy cape;
    Another, in pursuit,
    Tacked and turned about.

Yet never, when a sudden gust
Laid them together, could hold fast;
    They scarcely met before
    The wind got up once more.

Epiclesis

Come, yes, again come,
Holy One!
The possessed, serene,
frighten the
Untaken. We see
Heads wrenched back
By the long hair that
Lashes with
Such cruel strokes the
Wind of noon.
The wind holds that hair
In a strong
Grip. It is not free,
Though we may
See it float fiercely
As if free.

Nor are their bleeding
Lips, the black
Oozings on their cheeks,
Violence.
Those others lie still,
Cradled in
The storm they make. They
Buffet us
With their whirling, they
Deafen us
With unhearing cries,
It is we
Who taste the salt on
Bitten lips –
With that salt, may we
Be salted!

May we, by turning,
Wind ourselves
Tight into silence;
Cry ourselves
Holy, deaf as stones.
We do well
Not to hear what the
Unruly
Tongues, the bold bodies
Say to us.
Do we call, Dear Lord,
Out of love? –
Neither you nor we,
The master
Nor the mastered, could
Believe that.

Imperialists in Retirement

'I have done the state some service'
Othello

Tender each to the other, gentle
      But not to the world that has just now
Snatched back its gifts. Oh fallen, fallen
      From your proconsular state! I watch
Perhaps too closely, with too much
      Easy pity, the old man's loving
Protective gesture – the old woman
      Accepting the arms of a blind man,
Leaning upon it. I look around
      At the faded chintz, at china chipped
By so many packings, unpackings.

I listen, too. This part is not so
      Easy. He is not resigned. He cries
Aloud for the state he kept. He wants
      Privilege still and power, the long
Moonlit nights of the steamship voyage
      Out to a new appointment, whisky
And bridge and talk of what's to be done –
      The phrase again: 'They're children, really.'
And he beats with feeble hands against
      The immovable door of blindness,
The shut door of the years. 'Live in the
      Past,' he says. 'That's the thing. Live in the
Past.' And his wife soothes him, as one would
      A child when it's nearly his bedtime.
'One mustn't grumble,' she says. 'Times change.'

Her hands are reddened and swollen I
      Notice, saying goodnight. Her head shakes.
She stumbles a little in rising.
      Tonight she washes up. Tomorrow
She will scrub their kitchen on her knees.
      I see, as we go, the look of love
From her to him blind. Then the door shuts.

Pietà

(The Pietà of Villeneuve-lès-Avignon, in the Louvre)

An unstrung bow. The white, slack
Body collapsing. Mourners
Like mountains. And the tallest
Holds this: a forked, glistening
Glacier there is her lap.
Christ, I think, Christ. I don't know
Whether I swear or name. My eyes
Slip away, then again look
At the dead man, and then at
Mary, Mary Magdalen
And John. At last at the one
Modest and assured, who kneels
To the side.

           He stares right past
What's happening, though he paid
The painter to set it down.

The Barbarian Invasions

From distant Gaul the generals wrote how grave
Was the new threat; the common soldiers found
That they had lost the knack of being brave,

With every gap in harness made a wound
By thought. And waiting to be crossed,
There lay the frozen Rhine, and all the ground

Was hard and ringing with the iron frost.

The Link

I'm late tonight, and tired. We sit together
Under the white glare of the kitchen lamp,
Chipped plates and family silver on the table.
We eat the food you'd cooked, discuss the weather.
The questions start. It seems my weariness
Can draw you blindly. The familiar cramp
Of love that holds too closely makes me less
Kind than I should be. Dinner ends in trouble,
And I am pained to cause you this distress.

'What's to be done?' I ask a little later,
Alone now in my room. The bookshelves full
Of books you do not care for can't reply.
And then the phone rings with its steely stutter.
A friend's voice. In a moment I've discovered
Kindness enough. And yet I know the bell
Still stutters in your head as if unanswered.
No comfort for this curiosity
Grown great with love, that will not be delivered.

The Naming

(for Marisa)

It was not easy there. The wakening
Was not the worst. He rubbed his eyes. He saw
His own aloneness, separateness of being.
The apple tree hurled its thin shadows down.
His task was told him: 'Choose – your word God's law –
A name for everything that cries for one.'

All Eden cried. No part could say what sound
Matched its own inwardness. The whole of nature
Waited upon his word. Even the ground
Begged for a name, He touched it, called it 'earth'.
No plant must be forgotten, and no creature.
The names were born. A slow and painful birth.

Why did they tear at him, those names he made?
He could not tell. But each name meant a death,
Even before the apple. Choosing died
With every choice. In later years he'd say
Eden was perfect. That was not the truth.
He, if not she, was glad to go away.

The Wise Child

I couldn't wait. My childhood angered me.
It was a sickness time would cure in time,
But clocks were doctors slow to make me well.
I sulked and raged. My parents told me 'play' –
I stood in the garden, shouting my own name,
The noise enlarged me. I can hear it still.

At last I've come where then I longed to go.
And what's the change? – I find that I can choose
To wish for where I started. Childhood puts
Its prettiest manners on. I see the dew
Filming the lawn I stamped.
                                        The wise child knows
Not here, not there, the perfect somewhere waits.

To Be Justified

I suddenly wake. Some words. I grope for what
My dream was saying. Twisted blankets, sheets,
Bind me like my own entrails. Curtains swell,
Break wind, collapse. Next door a party pounds.
'I' shouts a voice. 'I. I…' The music swills
The rest of the sentence out and far away.
Then from my lost dream: *To be justified…*

                                        I lie here,
Turning the words about, these three cold pebbles.
Again sleep rises, tingling up each limb.

Vanitas

Which is also an allegory of the senses

Centred upon a mirror and a skull –
Inhabited only by a blackamoor.
His pink palm stretching out towards a bowl
Presents some bursting grapes, a gaudy flower.
There's dust on velvet, there is silence in
The shining belly of this violin.

Oh smell the flower – one weighty petal shed
And floating on the marble like a ship!
It stinks corruption. Rap the hollow head,
The chilling mirror with a fingertip.
All your diviners say divinity
Moves the hour-glass, crawls in what you see.

from
Towards Silence
(1968)

Adam and Tristan

How it echoes, echoes,
Sighs and repeats itself –
The voice of legend; the
Tale told, the instrument
Of telling. Tristan who
Takes the cup in his hand
And drains it. (They are on
The sea, coming from those
Black Kingdoms of Ireland.)
And Adam, to eastward,
Between two rivers, gnaws
The russet skin of the
Fruit of knowledge, while the
Beasts run loose, appetites
Now unappeasable.
Brute falls upon brute, to
Breed or to slaughter. Hear
Lamenting, rejoicing,
The voice that recounts it,
Shaped by the mouth, by the
Tongue and teeth of the brute.

Alteration

The fickleness of things –
The shed leaf, and the dropped
Banana skin. Things change
And we are altered – flat
On our backs, looking up
At the drilling squadrons
Of remote galaxies.

I send you a message
Star. Can words be lifted
Out, over light years, through
All the empty blackness?
They can. We are the two
Halves which make this event,
The high and the humble.

The point is to find it –
The way of being. Will
I ever yoke these stiff
And brittle bones to the
Rhythm I speak and speak of?
It is hard to be sure.
The heel slips, the leaf falls.

Christmas Snowfall

The whites of our eyes!
And then a random
Sprinkling of whiteness.
We look up. The snow
Falls, tangles in roots
Of eyelashes, melts
Into unmeant tears.

The angels in their
Long white nightdresses
Are beating their beds.
They shake their wings. It
Is the day when they
Waken, with great plumes
Gliding above us.

A few feathers that
Drift downwards, a few
Cries from the heavens.
Too fine! Too high! Yet
Something is nearer
And blesses. The time
Is weeping for us.

Fragment of a 'Tristan' – I

(an alternative version)

It was dark in the wood;
Tristan, a hungry beast,
Crouched in his hut of bark,

Shunning what sunlight came,
He gnawed a bloody bone,
ears full of the wind's roar.

Beside him lay Iseult,
Face pale, hair smeared with ash,
In tears sunk to the ground.

And neither heard King Mark
Who rode, with muzzled hounds
And bridle-bells cut off

Among the shouting trees,
His horse sunk to the hocks
In slime of rotten leaves.

Before the hut he stopped,
Let fall the reins and tugged
His right glove half way off.

And then he tugged it back.
He turned, and rode away,
And whistled as he went.

Fragment of a 'Tristan' – II

(Tristan's Madness)

The madman enters the gate,
Mocked by the boys of the town.
He is a sick wolf, a cur
In a rain of stones. The blood
Streams from his broken forehead.
Baffled, he trudges onward.
They bring him to the King's hall,
And the King says, 'Welcome, friend!'
And seats him a long way down.
'Why did you come here?' they ask,
And he tells them, 'My mother
Was a whale, and my old nurse
was a she-tiger; I have
A sister more beautiful
Than any woman living.
I must exchange her.' – 'And what
Will you take?' – 'Iseult, who is
Not so fine, but who will not
Keep me in danger of sin.'
And the grooms and the servants
Laugh so loud that the knights ask
Why, and the lords ask the knights
For the reason, and the King
Smiles, and calls to the madman,
'If I gave you Iseult, where
Would you take her, for women
Like to lie soft, and a queen
Must lie softer than any?'
– 'I have a hall of glass, lord,
High in the heaven, and light
Flows through it, and your Cornish
Winds do not shake it, and my
Harpers play music all night.
She would lie soft in my arms.'
And the company laughs again
At the folly of this fool.

Then Iseult comes in. She looks
Along the tables, and she sees,
Crouched in a corner, a man
In rags, eyes sunk, and forehead
Bloody. She bruises her lip,
So as not to cry, 'Madman!'
So as not to cry, 'Tristan!'

Gallipoli: Fifty Years After

on the pale sand of the beach
a bleached jawbone
                              two colours
the creamy white of bone the
changeable silver

                         listen
this bone is an oracle
the wave speaks in it
                              moving
up and over the sand

                              salt
I taste salt on my lip I
taste my own blood
                         or the sea
flowing with blood
                         I never
set foot here how long I have
been
            crawling from sea to land

fifty years

                    when the bullets
tore me my lungs filled with blood
the sea caught me received me
I fell back into what soft
imprisoning arms
                          the rifles
with leaden tears sprinkled the
water around me

                          but now
I have slept enough and must
climb towards shore
                                every
bone rolls from under the weed
presses up the weight that
the pebbles lay on it

                          they
will come when I call them
ribs
shake off that rotten webbing
skull
shed that crushed helmet

I command
I summon you all
                          a whole expedition
of bones

Genesis

1

The apple tasted of flesh. The
Blood of the apple was salt
(Though it smelt sweet, like semen).

Adam's mouth was choked with blood.
His flesh stiffly erect, like
The flesh of a hanging man.

The plan was written in this:
The superfluous part stood,
A tall monument to foresight.

2

The blackbird is a spy. And the
Magpie chatters. The jackdaw
        Is full of his tricks,
The squirrel is insolent,
        The cuckoo mocking.

What is to be seen, beneath
This tree? A beast with two backs.
        A beast which labours
With sowing and with ploughing.
        An apple, bitten.

3

Speech! Speech of the serpent!
What words? Syllables of
Ocean. Eve ripens,
Apple-rounded. Within
That belly, sibilant
Murmuring. The snake coils,
The wave shudders. And Cain
Waits his hour to be born.

Gran Tierra, Cuba

First the dry hills,
And then the wet.
The trees laden
With orchids, and
The greenness, the
Red of the earth
Whose dust robes me.
I am ready.
There is something
That must be said.
But what is it?
Where among all
These trees, these vines
Can I find it?
Where among those
Who lift their hands
To say 'welcome'?
Is it a voice
In the forest?
A knock in the
Heart? My own self
Speaking, or the
Whole land speaking?

Night falls. Far off,
Beyond the palms,
The sea breaks. It
Sings, there in the
Windward Passage,
A tune without
Audible words.

'Heureux Qui, Comme Ulysse…'

(for Polly Carnegie)

Happy he (or she)
Who travels the day
Hopefully, and the
World without hope, calm,
A smiling stoic
Who savours what his
Life may bring. Happy
The day of birth, and
Happy our dying;
Without that, life will
Not be known. Let all
Be seen for itself,
For what it is! Do
Not fear the voyage
Towards the world's edge
And the final hour.
Take pity on time.
Welcome each event
Because it greets you
As the destined one.

Looking at a Drawing

The line sets forth and
Wanders like a fox
Hunting. A blot falls
Here like a birdfoot.
This is like a man's
Steady striding round
The familiar paths
Of his own garden.
And this like the dragged
Belly of something
Wounded. The blood drops
Follow each other,
Hedgerow to hedgerow.
The mind follows that
Track. So many marks,
So many footprints
In the fields of snow.

'Oh To Be That Round O!'

Oh to be that round O!
The boomerang that soars
And returns to the hand;
The migrant bird, flying
Back to the same marshes
As the year moves onward.

'Here I am,' say the words,
In this place, at this time.
Unstable, not the round
Moon, but moon in water,
Shivering in the wind,
Shattered by one pebble.

Silence

Silence: one would willingly
Consume it, eat it like bread.
There is never enough. Now,
When we are silent, metal
Still rings upon shuddering
Metal; a door slams, a child
Cries; other lives surround us.

But remember, there is no
Silence within; the belly
Sighs, grumbles, and what is that
Loud knocking, that summoning?
A drum beats, a drum beats. Hear
Your own noisy machine, which
Is moving towards silence.

Spider Man

Surrounded, bound by
Many filaments
To fellow men, to
Other places, things –
I try to see. I
Touch, taste, spider-like
These trembling threads.
Not flies but feelings
Feed me. What buzzes,
Struggles in the web?
Is it full of juice
And blood? I run out
Along my ladders,
Jump from ambush, to
Seize the nourishing.

Tainted Fruit

Medlars, mulberries –
Half-rotten tainted
Fruit. The tongue savours
The rot. I gorge on
Pulp and juice, stain lips
With doubtful colour.
And the mind rejects
This fleshly greed, broods
On what pleases it:
The melancholy
That it hopes to find,
How quickly the weed
Spreads over the pond!
And how the blight runs
Over the green leaves!
All's dim, corrupt. See,
We must pander now
To appetite, and
What the flesh desires.

Teeth and Bones

Teeth and bones. How it
Curls its lip, the earth-
Eater, sucks the pebbles
And then spits them out!
The sea mumbles, and
Here is the hard word
It cannot pronounce:
Finitude, the name
Of certainty. Chew
These again, and suck
Till the bones are bare.
They are bones still, and
They are always there.

The Bureaucrat

Master of the jot,
And of the tittle,
Of precedent, of
Forms simple or not;
Proconsular, yet
Careful of pins and
Paper-clips. 'It all
Depends,' you say, but
Will never tell us
On what. The wheel turns,
Thanks to your shoulder.
Culture continues.
To any purpose?
The question goes
Outside your brief. You
Must write a memo
On that, endorse it,
And send it higher.

The Drowning Dream

The drowning dream, the
        long way down –
at first the sun gleams
        like a red
eyeball staring at
        this tiny
light thing, my drowning
        body which
twirls in the current.
        I forget
the sun later, and
        just drown. I
breathe the searing salt,
        choke on it.
And I wake choking.

The Researcher

Consuming a green
World and content
With what I consume, worm
On a leaf and part
Of a universe
That is all cabbage,
What I know, I am.
I move without mind
Through things of the mind,
Always eating. Holes
Show where I have been.
If I met the fly
I exist to make
I should only ask:
'Can that be eaten?'
I leave behind me
More space, more nothing,
More dust, less cabbage.

Three Songs for Surrealists

1 *For René Magritte*

An eye is watching
From my plate –
There's someone here
I almost ate.

The spinach-fed
Are often wrong;
More strength than brain,
But brains are strong.

The room is full,
No place for us;
An apple is
An octopus.

2 *For Max Ernst*

A nightingale
As big as a house
Swallowed a man
As small as a mouse:

Sweet sweet sweet
Cried the nightingale,

Under the feathers
Lost in the dark
The man was frightened
And started to bark:

Bow wow wow
Cried the nightingale.

And the moon looked down
With a chilly stare
At the woods and the bird
Who was barking there:

Hear me now
Cried the nightingale.

Why should a man
Inside of a bird
Bark like a dog –
Isn't that absurd?

Oh not so
Cried the nightingale.

3 *For Salvador Dali*

We sleep. The earth
Shakes. The thunder
Murmurs to us.
We sink deeper
And deeper still
Into the dream.

When I lay down
The world changed. It
Rocked like water
Struck by a stone,
Ripples spreading
To shake my dream,

Nightmares. Sainthoods.
The sky-trellis.
Emblems of love.
Signs of terror.
What is a man
But his own dream?

Your Own Place

Invent it now, your own place,
Your own soil. All inferior
Localities are done with.
Yet how is it to be made
Without things remembered? Sun
Thrown in fistfuls, and the sand
Of that ripe apricot; wind
Spiced with thyme and lavender
Blowing from one hill, at one
Season. But these bring with them
Disasters – the imperfect
Friendship broken, and the perfect
Love unconsummated. Sand
Which burns the foot, hill blocking
The view. So invent it now,
And arrive after the long
Voyage, alone, having left
A companion at each
Port, a lover in all the
Hot bedrooms, all the stifling
Cabins.

       It is before dawn.
There is a cove with a few
Bare rocks. Your feet cling to them
Naked, as the rest of you
Is naked. Women come laughing
Down to the shore. You call out,
Expecting to be embraced.
They strip and bathe, brush by you
Without a glance or a cry
As the light swells and brightens.

from
The Well-Wishers
(1974)

An Epitaph

(reconstructed from Posidippus)

Here in this rough trench lies,
Wrapped in his shroud – the rags
Which served as his best coat –
One Phyromachus, the
Poor tattered glutton who,
Like a bedraggled crow,
Hung hopefully about
At midnight revels. Please
Anoint his stone and put
Some flowers there if you
Ever in the small hours
Were joined by a such a man.
From the Lenean games
He came, with broken teeth,
Black eyes, a bloody pate
(The oil-flask in his hand
Was everything he owned),
And, drunk, fell in this hole:
A tragi-comic fate.

Asleep

Alexander smelt of violets,
And you of vanilla. My tongue,
Touching some part of you, forearm
Or nipple, tells me you are salt,
And yet your odour still rises,
Powerfully sweet. Paradise
Of my imagination!
Thickets, bowers, crevices! Paths
Twined and retwined, going nowhere!
In your veins there are nightingales;
In your bowels, hyenas. Cries
Reach me from those you long ago
Devoured, all but their voices.
Softly, with tongue-tip and finger
I follow the clues you have left.
The little hairs stand up. You groan,
Hugging your dream and contented.
What do you mean me to find? You
Withdraw into sleep and won't answer –
Present and solid beside me,
Further and further receding.

At Forty

Imprisoned night! Black space within me,
In which a child's voice cries: 'I am still
You! Still the true you! Fears and desires,
Perhaps concealed, but ruling as before!'
Look outside the window. There a tree
Is pumping sap. Time kills but feeds. I
Add a ring to make my double score.

Bamboo Shoots

Today your bamboo shoots
Are not to your liking. They
Were gathered after the sun
Rose, and on the wrong mountain.
I should have ordered better
Weather. The record I hoped
Would soothe you is yesterday's
Favourite. You sit in the
Best armchair and glare at me.
Every line of you says:
'Do something! Send to China
For bamboo shoots. Stop me
From being so unhappy.'
The furniture sulks; curtains
Are full of melancholy.
Poor love, poor lover. It is
No comfort to you to say
I would rather be here and
Gloomy because of your gloom
Than laughing with another.

Beds

Nothing more tell-tale
Than beds we have
Made love in. Darkness
Illuminated;
What was closed, opened.
Sated, we get up.
The bed bears witness
Of how we fell deep
Each into other.

Descending

(for Bridget Riley)

Going down. How the voice
Stepwise descends. Who cries
There behind the curtain,
And says those muffled words –
Unintelligible
Secrets being told?
You would like to know them.
But if you heard clearly
Would you not invoke the
Black descent of silence?

Lovers

Et ego confiteor! tua sum nova praeda, Cupido;
porrigimus victas at tura iura manus.

Ovid: *Amores*, I, ii

1

Clothes on a chair, torn off
Pell-mell, in the hurry
To be joined, and get to
Our business. Lax, slack
Pieces of cloth, the shed
Husk that the world looked at.
The constructed being
So lightly got rid of,
I marvel at all the years
Spent making it. But
Later, dressing, I see
How we are both transformed,
That the material
Clingingly moulds us, and
The voice and face alter
As the armour fastens.

Locked, rocking together
In the animal act,
Limbs tensed, mouthing the old
Banned ritual words... Soon
Memory will soften
The harshness of loving.
Our bodies will slip, roll
Numbly apart, hands linked
Perhaps, or thighs brushing
One over another.
These are the times we hold
Easily in mind: not
The immediate, hard
And dangerous minute,
When the self drowns, and the
Stifled cry wrenches out.

3

Someone else's sweat, still
Pungent on the pillow.
The sheets rumpled; each fold
Seeming to remember
The act that created it.
I lie upon a chart,
A record of movements,
Intertwinings, knottings
Of limbs. And our whispers
Have died in the hollow
Dark of the room. Absence...
Then the blackness fills up.
You people it; your selves,
Guessed at, are around me.
My hands reach out, surprised
That they do not find you.

4

No sooner over, the
Partner gone, the flesh still
Wrenched and weary, than a
Voice begins and images
Burn on the screen of the
Closed eyelid. To be thus,
And thus. The bowels shake
With impossibly wild
Spasms, and the fibres groan.
Now, waking in the dawn,
I am calmer, and have
Time to listen to the
City which moves towards
Another part of its
Cycle. And there, far off,
The crowing of a cock.

5

The ghost of your body
Clings implacably to
Mine. When you are absent,
The air tastes of you, and
Last night the sheets had your
Texture. Then, when I looked
In this morning's mirror,
I found a bruise which had
Suddenly risen through
The milky flesh, a black
Star on the breast, surely
Not pinned there before (I
Count my wounds, and record
The number). How did it
Arrive? The ghost made it.
I turn, hearing you laugh.

6

The body burning bright
Like a light bulb. Fever
Thinning its substance. I
Do not know if the flesh
Shines because of what we
Did together, but the
Heat of fever is now
Entirely yours, your own
Ambassador, as if
You filled my veins with a
Reminder; as if, too,
My blood became yours – I
Keep it on sufferance
Only. Make a cut and
Let it drain out. You
Rise from the red, embodied.

7

The rain falls in strings, beads
To be counted. It wears
Out the night and the rock:
All things succumb to it.
I cannot tell if time
Is being washed away,
Or if this is time, made
Tangible as water.
My fever has returned,
Like an icy river.
In bed alone, I am
Dissolving. Flesh becomes
Like the wet sacks out there
Abandoned in the dark
Of the garden, lapsing
Slowly into the earth.

Ah, how I want to make
Every inch of skin,
Each muscle and organ
Mine! My name, thought of, or
Casually spoken,
Must seize your joints. Any
Hint of my presence must
Bring dryness to the tongue,
A cracking of knuckles.
Let these be the signals
That travel between us.
Do not ask if they go
Already from you to
Me. The hand shakes, forming
The words of the poem.

North-West Passage

(for Birgit Skïold)

White ocean, white
Sky mingling with it;
The pack-ice grumbling
Like a skull that grins
What teeth are left. And
In the hidden dark
Of icy water
The seal-god crooning
To the voyager:
'Come to me! Come down!
Leave one page clean of
Steps, one blank unspoilt,
Some whiteness in this
Scribbled-over world!'

On Blackness

(for Basil Beattie)

A void wherever
His hands reach. His eyes
Shuttered, and even
His nostrils breathing
An ebony smoke.
Tongue that tastes nothing.

Wrapped in blackness, a
Man trembles, alone
In midnight's meadow,
The whole universe
Suddenly removed,
All its candles snuffed.

On Light

(for Barry Martin)

The voyager that
Travels the furthest:
Light, ambassador
Of all that we find
Most remote from us
(Slowly pulsing, the
Brightness of a star).

It is the nearest
We get to knowing
How the world moves, what
Grips it, what forces
Impel it towards
The last boundary
At the end of light.

Postcard

Don't get hurt in my world
Of shared jokes and easy
Betrayals. They are all
Ambitious where I
Come from: many hide it
Better than I. Enjoy
The explosions and
Sky-rockets and the tunes
Of my poems, but the
Truth they bring you is truth
As oracles tell it.
A poet of my kind
Skates on the thinnest ice.

Snow Poem

Hold out your linked hands,
Lovers, that the snow
May tell your fortune.
See how it melts! You
Are too hot for it.
Love too will leave you,
If not as quickly.
Oh come indoors now
To the sheets' whiteness:
Flakes tap on the pane,
Moths in the darkness.

The Dawn Ray

Now dawn is filtering between
The roughly drawn curtains. Not yet
Fully appeased, we begin our
Approaches. Stealthy, a hand moves
From nipple to belly, fingers
Test for an opening. Sighing,
You signal; sighing, I answer.
We cannot help it, but like two
Twigs we come drifting together,
Borne away once more by the stream,
Rocking and being rocked in spasm
On spasm. How easy to hate you,
Dear love, for what I do in this
Pale ray of light that crosses our
Struggling bodies, gripped in a
Death-lock, devouring each other.

The Interview

Visit to an old poet with a young wife:
Hammering in the kitchen, children
Shouting in the yard, a breeze that blows
To flutter the curtains, slam the doors.
He's willing to talk, in his second
Harvest, which is also his new spring
(Verse pushing the flagstones up and tongue
Running free as the pen). He gives me
Whisky to see if I can drink, tells
A dirty story or two. Bang, bang –
They're putting up shelves, and laughing,
The young wife and the young man with her.
'Joe can't write,' she says, as we eat our
Food. 'There are other jobs he can do.'

The Photograph

Click! And the light slips past
The shutter. One of your
Expressions sticks to
The film as if it were
Flypaper. It halts at
This moment in time while
The world is hurtling on.
Click! I have stolen one
More fragment of your life,
To be looked at later,
In a different mood
Perhaps and without your
Presence. I notice how
Uneasy I make you,
Shuffling prints like a pack
Of playing cards. Lost selves,
Delivered to me, not yours
Any longer. *Click! Click!*
You would like to hold the
Light back, prevent it from
Entering the lens. You
Feel yourself being dragged
With it like a man drawn
Into a whirlpool. You
Are afraid of this small
Black prison, and think you
May never escape. *Click!*
The snick of a lock. Yet
It is merely time past
You leave with me. I hold
What you once were: only
A second ago, a
Day by the time the print
Comes back, or a year by
The time I take it out
Of a drawer, and look,
And say: 'That was when we
Were happy and did not
Know it.' *Now smile please! Click!*

The Son

Lying awake, in the room
Over their room, the voices
Drifting up through the floorboards –
A grinding, night-long quarrel
Between the two who made you.
How can you bear to listen?

A shared life, a shared hatred
To warm it in the small hours.
Four living children, one dead.
Five proofs of something, one you
Who lie there above them. Grey
Coals hiss as the fire burns low.

The Well-Wishers

(for Patric Dickinson)

Most often in broad daylight:
A white cloak swaying at a
Street corner; stillness at noon
As, somewhere a long way off,
Thunder mutters a promise.
Or, on a country journey,
From the dusty hill behind,
The flash of a mirror, held
In a watcher's hand. Smoke-trails
Ahead, in the thick pinewoods.
But even at night, in sleep,
There are always signs. Do they
Ever drowse, the well-wishers?
Or do they sometimes merely
Hold those cloaks before their faces,
Hoping to conceal from us
Their next move, the full extent
Of their good intentions?

Touching

Tonight I touch, and you too
Touch; the flesh slides gently
Over the bare flesh. Fingers
Walk the gradient of a
Spine and count each bone; the beads
Shifting as they are counted.

We read the body's braille, and
How it sings to the blind touch!
We are devoured by touching;
Arms and thighs, moving against
And yet together! Our hands
Following a scent like hounds!

Our edges blur. We soften
And melt outward. Becoming
Part of what we touch, become
A new existence. Snow and
Fur, each with a different
Softness. Metal. And your bones.

Translated to Translator

(for Alain Bosquet)

Two pasts for you, kind
Colleague, one for me.
For at each step your
Language makes you know
If what is said to
Happen, happens once,
Or is repeated. See –
I say I loved. How
Durable was love?
Your tenses, downright,
Tell if loving was
A single moment
Or a chain of days.
Worse still with pronouns.
For who was loved, a
'She' or else a 'he'?
My slippery tongue
Equivocates on
Persons, as on times.
For this, then, thanks, that
Through my Channel fogs
You still pursue – but
Are they there to find? –
Elusive truth, and
Simple poetry.

Drinking Irish, that was your
Grandmother: a Catholic
Rollicking in puritan
Wales. Drunk or sober, disliked
Your father – no love between
Those two. St Patrick's Night was
The night for drinking, of all
The drinking nights of the year.
Drunk she came home and missed the
Bucket; pissed on the floor and
Stained the ceiling, a map of
Ireland for those below.
                              Dad
Said: 'Leave it. Teach the bitch a
Lesson.'
              Left it was, for year
After year. Grandmother died.
That ceiling remembered her;
Father still hated her noisy
Ghost. Then, six months back, he said:
'Repaint it! Why must we live
With the old bag's mark?' You were
Silent, thinking: 'Poor father,
Cleaning up, ready to go.'

Uncollected Poems
(1974–1995)

A Former Lover

It's ten years since I heard, and
Then one day a letter comes.
It's neutral stuff, until I
Delve into the envelope
Again and find your photo,
Handsome still, and not a line
To tell me why you sent it.
A week, a fortnight passes.
Now, one night, the phone, with 'Guess
Who this is?' I do at once,
And sense the link that joins our
Lives, as they were joined before,
And see you naked, open
To my touch. What did I say?
That making love with you was
Like being asked to play
A violin, untutored,
Which taught me its own music.
Enough. Enough. The reason
Why we parted has not changed.
We liked each other's bodies –
Flesh more attuned than spirit.
Indeed, we are closer now,
Remembering might-have-beens,
Planning to meet, and knowing,
As we say it, it won't be.

A Happy Snap

Here is my girlfriend, Happy Lil.
She had a taste for sun and fun,
And bathing in the nude, until,
Alas, one day she was undone.

I was about to snap her thus,
Last summer, from the beach at Rhyll,
When up there swam an octopus
Who made advances to my Lil.

'Oh rescue me, dear Alf!' she cried.
'Oh don't desert me in my trouble!
I'll give my all, if you'll provide
A helping hand…' One final bubble.

How could I save her? Don't forget
I would have got my camera wet.

Azaleas

(for Polly)

More familiar to me
Than wayside plants poets are
Supposed to sing of – the bright,
Scentless hothouse blooms with which
We brighten winter in towns.
Pink and white azaleas
You brought me for my birthday!
When I look at them, their leaves
Now falling, and the blossoms
Fading at the tops of the stems,
I hear the music of *Manon*:
'*Adieu, petite table!*' – theatre
Crowded, and audience rapt.
The pleasure of cities! These plants
Remind me of what they miss
Who shun our rainy streets, and
Midnight conversations.

'Blackbirds are Eating...'

Blackbirds are eating the elderberries
Before they have ripened.

The thing is to find something
You want to return to.

Early pleasures taste sour
Compared to what comes later.

Already in August
A leaf turns in my garden.

I'm hurrying to find words
For a time not arrived at.

Clothing

One has to slough off
That carapace
Of acquired habits
And known locutions.

The sirens whose mouths must be stopped
Are long-term guests
In the inner ear.
Their tones seem to mimic one's own
But they are in fact
Those whom one mimics.

What's left seems pitifully little –
Chapped, scraped, rubbed raw
By the struggle to shed
What feels like skin
But is only clothing.

Crystal Ball

A trap for light, drawing
All rays towards itself,
Gathering together
Broken rainbows, able
To give transparency
Back to the muddied flow.
Put this in a stream, with
Ripples rushing past it:
All the flotsam, ashamed
Of its own nature, shrinks
Back to the bank, leaving
The water to rival
This sovereign clearness.
But look again, and see
How, trapped within the sphere,
Is not light alone, but
A little universe,
Inverted, in all things
Opponent, opposite.

Dancing

You were dancing, your eyes shut
So tightly against the lights
And all of the people watching
How you moved to the music.
And I danced with you, my bold
Eyes too fixed on your shut face,
Willing you to open those lids,
And look at me, and let me look
All the way into you, where
Our real dance moved, sure of
Itself and unceasing.

Eclipse

Like the shadow
Eating the sun's disc,
A poem
Gradually obscures
The event that sets it in motion.
It does not make clear,
It makes dark.

What transparency
One feels in that darkness –
The hand one holds out
Vanishes.
First flesh, then bones melt.
The sense of touch diffuses
Throughout the universe,
One touches and is touched by everything
Until the eclipse passes.
Too soon.

Five Morsels in the Form of Pears

(for William Scott and Erik Satie)

1

Personal problem: how to
Get over that wall and sink
My teeth into a beauty?
The orchard is a harem –
Swelling hips and large bottoms.
You can almost hear them, those
Female conversations
About their jewels and children,
About their seeds and raindrops,
New life and how to make it.

2

That black-and-yellow buzzing –
A nest of guards to punish
The intruder. Swollen with
Stings, you'll regret your boldness.
Ah! the pain of the half-shut
Wounded eye that looked too close
At imprisoned love! It is
Not like that. Every wasp
Is choosing a bride, palping
Flesh and savouring juices.

3

They are courting their tethered
Victims, who hang by a stem
Between air and earth, between
Growing and dying. The wasps
Walk on the surprisingly
Chapped skin, and then probe and probe.
You expect a convulsive
Movement, a tiny outcry
As virginity is lost
While the wound opens, oozes.

4

How swift the transition
From favourite to mother!
You would not care, now, for what
This broadhipped woman offers:
A family of grubs in
An impassive form which has
Passed in a moment from ripe
To rotten. You did not come
In time. 'It is all over,'
She says, meaning her sweetness.

In another part of the
Orchard, and hanging from a
Different tree; or perhaps
On a plate on a table,
Squatting there half-tilted and
Content to wait. It arrives,
The moment of decision.
They know they are fortunate
To be thus summoned, looked at,
Picked for the preservative
Violations of art.

Gone

Giving you up is like
Losing a bad habit,
Nose-picking, nail-biting,
The dull solace of my
Unoccupied moments.
One has to be alert
Or an absence pricks one.
Don't wonder what it was
That filled the space between
Thinking and thinking.
                              Gone.
My day is like a staircase
Which has one step missing.

Holbein's Lady With a Squirrel

Mildly she waits. The painter, hair by hair,
Fills in the details of her ermine cap,
The way the light turns on her squirrel's fur.
The betting is, she doesn't care a rap
For all this fuss. So let the artist stare –
She will not catch his glance, but looks away,
Thinking of sheets to iron and cakes to bake:
Duties she loves, not just for their own sake
But for their repetition, day by day.
Let Holbein finish soon, there's much to do.
Like him she has a world she must renew.

In California

'I can't sleep,' you say, alone
In California.
I catch my breath and murmur
Platitudes without comfort.
Looking out of my window
I see the grey daylight
Of a January noon.
For you day's not begun yet –
Hot asphalt, dusty palm trees.
I reach out along the wire,
Trying to say this to you:
'Come back when you are ready,
But be ready, or we are
More divided.' Lack of love
In the same bed separates
Further than all the thousands
Of miles from my day to your
Night, sleepless and accusing.

In Secret

Yes, I write this poem in
Secret, not from you, but from
Myself. Look, I say, I have
Escaped your black art, words mean
Just what they say, and no more.
Yet my notebook calls. Someone
Is late, the mind is idle.
I scribble, chaotic strokes
Scarcely creating letters.
Let us pretend this is
Not happening, a poem
Is not being born. The spell
Is not cast or, if it is,
Has nothing to do with love,
Dearest love, nothing at all.

Inscriptions

I

The dry clink of the chisel.
White dust falling. What shall I
Write on the innocent stone?
Noble words, to subdue the
Wilful veins in the marble?
No – let stone speak of being
Stony. So many aeons
To achieve the hardness that
The steel now flouts. Oceans
That fled. Sediments, age-long
Deposits. I need a tone
So quiet, so low only
Ears of marble can hear it.

II

Hidden in withering weeds,
The letters mossy, begrimed –
Memorial to what or
Whom? Beating the nettles down,
I stumble near, decipher,
With finger pressed against stone,
A name, a date. They are gone,
The person, the day, the year.
What lesson comes from the lost
And yet enduring text? One –
That 'all flesh is grass'. Of course,
This too can be read upon
The slab which is leaning here.

III

Cogwheels, flywheels, belts, pulleys –
Cacophony of machines
In motion. No point of
Rest, no possible moment
Of quiet. Set up a stone,
A pillar of black granite.
Write with a ringing hammer
An inscription on it.
Something, perhaps, of this sort:
'Reader, this is no common
Commemoration. Touch
The cold but singing surface.
One inch within lies silence.'

IV

Runes on a headland. Seagulls
That fight the wind. The old north
Still upstanding, a phallus
Ready to rip time's womb,
To impregnate the future
With its own bloodlust. Heroes
Shouting, biting their shield-rims,
Throwing their axes up. A
Hacked stone commemorates their
Berserk courage. Epic themes!
But blood can be shed with none
Of this hullabaloo. Not
Here, but elsewhere, it still flows.

V

Hieroglyphs. Calendars for
Unknown festivals. The light
Falls upon cut stone, healing
Its wounds. But the scarred boulder
Refuses to return itself
To the natural chaos.
It displays in the sunshine
The signs men have made on it,
Those badges of dishonour.
Not joined to mankind,
Nor yet aloof, it is null
But not void; neither wholly
One thing, nor yet the other.

VI

Sly answers to the concrete –
Hearts, arrows, initials,
Four-letter words. The city
Stammers its confessions
In these swarming graffiti.
KROPOTKIN LIVES is written
Beside a bridge; REMEMBER
ATTILA in the toilet
Of a major museum,
And beside this I SUCK COCK
In another handwriting.
Anonymous desires find
Their durable monuments.

VII

The design printed on the
Swelling bicep. Those hearts and
Flowers, dragons and daggers.
The fidelity of ports
Where the young man sits, half-drunk,
In the tattooist's parlour,
Sleeve rolled up, elbow planted
Firm on the table. The blood
Blossoms under the goad of
The moving needle. Years pass.
Now the old man cannot think
Who the girl was or where known,
Although his flesh remembers.

VIII

Written upon glass, written
Upon water. Transparent
Words. Lies! You can see through them!
Examine the letters of this
Inscription, find beneath
It another, another.
Who is to say what is the
Last, the ultimate message?
Water shifts, glass may shatter.
Not lies – provisional
Knowledge. The syllables
Move, and create the song of
Water falling, glass ringing.

IX

A stone, root-scribbled. Notebook
Of quiet ambitions –
The sly plan made by the grass
To grow higher, and water's
Project to flow. Unfulfilled,
All of them, because the page
Resists whatever it records.
Last summer, the grass died
Just where the stone lay. Last spring,
The water divided, just
Where it was. Stone overcame
All that lipping and lapping.
'Who tries next?' it says. 'Come on!'

X

A comet inscribing heaven –
Presage of change. Heads are to
Roll, regimes will be struck down
By deity's thunderbolts.
It looks so calm, the great arc
Of distant fire, transforming
The night sky into a stage
Where one show-off star displays
Its talent for entrances.
What a gift its author has
For flamboyant metaphors!
Some other messenger – a
Mere ant – could have brought us word.

'It's the Season for Broken Hearts'

It's the season for broken hearts.
The trees in the park stripped bare,
The streets sordid
With old cans, broken bottles,
Yellowed newspapers reporting
Those glorious days last year
Before our fates collided.
We sit home and examine our hurts
To see if they are still hurting,
And wait for the phone call
That will resume our war –
Dominance and submission,
The silences of battle
As each waits for the other
To announce a new position.
Then a bird chirrups 'Why bother?'
On a branch no longer naked.
A stranger comes to the door
With the necessary gift of danger.

Klee's Angels

I *Angel in the Making*

How does one make an angel?
See, on the paper, how the lines assemble.
Not quite meeting, not quite making
The form that gives being.
Or is it not so simple?
Does one see here
Something impossible,
An immortal dissolving,
Becoming nothing?

How hard it is
To bring the lines together
When one knows
(When one suspects)
The angel being made
Is the shape of one's own dying.

II *Angel Still Groping*

It stirs about
Like a sea-creature
At the bottom of a pool.
It tries to tear aside
The veils of colour
Wherein I entrap it.
As it breaks through one
My brush weaves another.
It will never reach me,

Yet it is strong, this angel,
Iron-limbed,
Harsh and hungry,
Ready to swallow
Whatever it is offered.
It wants to be fed –
That much is certain.
If it breaks through
This last veil of the spectrum
It will take me down
Into its own element.

III *Forgetful Angel*

Sometimes they forget.
Sometimes they turn away –
But seldom, seldom.
It is true that I have seen them
Knotting the corners
Of their white nightdresses
To keep in mind
A task still to be done.
I have seen them knot their fingers
In the effort to remember.

Always it comes back:
The telephone number,
Which house in the street
They were told to go to,
Which bell to press,
What name to ask for.

IV *Angelus Militans*

One can only draw it
As a child would,
Keeping the lines uncertain,
The shapes clumsy –
Two rolling eyeballs,
And a coy simper.

It will complain about the likeness
But enter into
The crippled and crippling
Image of itself.
This keeps it from being dangerous.
One is able to converse with it.

What one asks, of course,
Are a child's questions:
'What day will it be?
What will happen after?'

V *Angel Still Female*

It is wrong to unsex them,
although they encourage it –
white uniforms,
badly-made wings,
flaming swords.
How can one guess,
at a first approach,
that these are female,
and thus flirtatious?

A bunch of flowers,
a bag of sweets,
a lying word –
soon each of them is smiling.

Then one begins to beckon.
'Follow,' she says,
'follow me
into the wood,
down to the ocean.'

One dare not disobey.
One goes slowly,
just as slowly as one can,
scattering their portraits
like messages behind one.

Night Music

Cobblestones, doorways and
Jukeboxes. The posters
Show blonde beauties with
Raindrops on their nipples.
My coat is soaked through by
The evening downpour.
Why am I here? Better
To have stayed in the cold
Hotel room, listening
To the clatter of heels
and dishes. The wet dreams
That wake me trembling are
No worse than this hunt for
A lost scent, rank, musky,
And an eye that meets mine
Amid the night music.

Pan and Echo

Pan, hairy-thighed and goat-footed,
Roaming the valleys and foothills
Low down on Olympus, need
Stiffening his prick, clouding
His brain, each emission
A momentary release
From the bondage of Eros...

Where is he now? I see him,
In sunlight, flexing his thighs
At Mediterranean
Street corners. His nymphs descend
Giggling from aeroplanes, their
Ice-chip eyes scanning the locals
In search of the ultimate
Orgasm. These are easy lays who
Drive hard bargains.

Oh Echo!
Echo! He pursues you in markets,
He exposes his parts by the roadside. Every time
Your eye falls on that blunt paw
Groping his fly, your own thighs
Moisten. Turn away quickly,
Don your sunglasses, haggle
For tourist pots. You know he
Is watching still.

She is seized
With panic, Pan's own terror.
She cuts short her tour, changes
Her ticket, departs for her
Nordic fastnesses.

Now on
Winter mornings her fingers
Tickle her typewriter, 'Sir,
In reply to yours of the
14th inst...' She nods and dreams
Of a rough, hairy, half-animal
Creature, breath filling a set
Of reed pipes. The melody
Steals into her reluctant
Ears, makes her innermost self
Vibrate. She looks up from the
Keyboard and silently cries,
Mouth shaped in a tortured O:
'Have pity, terrible Lord!
Release your grieving Echo!'

Poems for Clocks

(for Wendell Castle)

I

Time's both the tortoise and the hare –
It leaps in front, it lags behind;
And those who try to grasp it find
It always has another where.

II

The clock kills all,
But keeps alive,
Dangling upon a fraying rope,
Two things: past joy,
And future hope.

III

Some come with tick,
And some with tock,
The seconds tumbling
From this clock.

They fall to rise –
A golden heap
Which buries even
Time in sleep.

IV

This clock, a good
Ventriloquist,
Matches the pulse
Within your wrist,
And thus gives speech,
Although apart,
To every movement
Of your heart.

V

Time moves no cogwheels,
Strikes no bell,
Keeping its own
Unsteady pace,
Capriciously
It drags or flies.
Therefore be loath
To trust this face:
What can clocks tell
But honest lies?

VI

Pity the labour of this beast
That night and day, and day and night,
Goes round its threshing floor of hours,
Blind to the darkness and the light.

VII

Imagine, then, a butterfly
Which strikes a boulder with its wing.
It splits the rock. Time passes by,
So light, and yet so shattering.

VIII

Imprisoned in the conjurer's room
Which swells and shrinks, your fear is great.
The windows mist, the mirrors loom,
The curtains stir to suffocate.

Then, as you draw your breath to shout,
You hear the clock in darkness chime,
A charm to drive the nightmares out –
The lullaby of passing time.

'Sleepily Murmuring...'

Sleepily murmuring, not
Certain as yet what manner
Of pleasure this is, or if
It is part of your dream or
The waking to come, you turn,
Arrange yourself, and accept
The sensation. And I,
Uncertain, not of the act,
But whether I've been given
Permission to enter
And mingle myself with what
You are dreaming, advance
Like a child in a game, two steps
Forward, one back, until I
Am sure of a welcome. You
Open your eyes, suddenly,
And I am caught out, stumble,
Drown in the turbulent blue.

Sparrows

They quarrel when the light
    Awakes them, and they curse
At the approach of night.
    They hate the universe.

Sometimes I think they are just
    Echoes of our own life,
Squabbling there in the dust,
    Perpetually at strife.

The Lagoon

(for Alejandro Obregòn)

And man divided the waters,
Cut off the conversation
Between salt and sweet, between
Landward and seaward. The lagoon
Could no longer unite mountains
And deeps, each giving a little
Of their secret essence. The fish
Knew it. The birds knew it. The plants
Above and below also knew it.
So they did what they could – they died:
Their way of saying that those who
Did this were from them (divided).

The Outcry

Oaks and beeches, but not one
Leaf strikes against another;
No trill of tongue from the
Innumerable birds. I
Can sense them gripping the twigs,
Holding with scaly rigour
The boughs where the sap rises
Silent in its flowing.
                       Then
Suddenly the heart hammers,
The leaves like shaken metal
Roar, and all the birds cry out.

The Welcome

Tongue to tongue, and limb
To limb. In the midst
Of making love, I
Am seized by the spasm
The past brings with it.
Histories: my life
Returning; shadows,
Unknown quantities
Perceived in you.
                       No.
This is the moment
To admit the rights
Of the mere surface.
My hand glides over
Rib-cage, then breast-bone.
The gesture bids you:
'Welcome, dear stranger.'

Things of this World

World that the wind caresses,
Spinning upon your pivot
In a cloak of clouds, in
Fanciful, leaf-stitched garments,
Shaking the birds from your sleeves
When the hour comes for the change
From one to the next season –
How can you be so mundane?
Yet that is your world, your own
And essential nature:
To be ordinary, to
Nurse our occupations.

Out in the garden. I look
And see the cloud as it goes,
The birds migrating, the leaf
That unfurls or falls. So dull,
So quotidian, and thus,
Always, packed with wonder.

Undressing

Stripping off, peeling, shucking –
Getting ready to offer
(With so many half-muttered
Shame-faced excuses) yourself.
How could I refuse you now?
The heat in the room is not
Merely the fire or the drink.
It rises up from my heart.
I love you for making this gift,
Though now it is mine I am
No longer perfectly sure
That I truthfully want it.
And yet how touching they are,
These small unknown details
Which enter the stage one by
One. A mole. A gold chain. A
Nipple. A scar. I number
Them gratefully now, the small
Tokens – now it is over.

Velasquez's An Old Woman Cooking Eggs

Before being cabined up within the court,
I painted these from Seville, cook and boy.
How strangely far it seems, the teeming town!
Here in these quiet rooms, Philip and I
Murmur of Spain's defeats. I use my art
As consolation for a fading king,
Painting his ghostly likeness once again,
Or else some dull-eyed dwarf or gibbering clown
Who made him smile once.
                              Here, it's all extremes,
Absolute power, absolute idiocy.
I paint them well, whatever it is I see,
But houses and streets of Seville haunt my dreams,
The common life forever lost to me.

Welsh Weather

Is there a book, where each
Page alters as soon as
One has read it? You are
Merlin shape-shifting high
In the mountains of Wales:
Now hawk, now hare, now a
Fish in the ringing stream,
Now suddenly a stone
In the path, to make me
Stumble and fall headlong.
A peal of thunder! The
Wizard's wrathful outcry,
Or just the Welsh weather?

Uncollected Poems
(1995–2001)

A Letter Home

Dear friends,
Do I really want
To be so much part
Of your consciousness?

Analysed in newspapers,
Pushed in front of television cameras?

Not now.
Not at all.
Please excuse me.

I do of course
Have an appetite for such things,
Which can be satisfied,
Out of your reach,
On remote frontiers.

Less risk,
And more solace,
May be found elsewhere
By me, who was once told,
Exiting the airport,
'You know, you are the most
Famous critic
In Buenos Aires.'

A Little Ode

(for Tom)

One door slams,
Another opens.
Things happen
In ways we cannot know.
How did we come to where we stand
On mountaintop,
In valley,
High or low?
Is there some turning clockwork
We obey?
Or do we have a say
In all this wandering?
Can we be sure,
Amidst our blundering,
That we're self-guided?
Or are we the derided
Toys of fate?
That's not the thing to ask.
Life gives us its own task.
What one asks is:
How did it taste?
Did it bring dark or light,
Joy or fright,
Gain or waste?
How went the day?

Affair

He looms above her.

Her knickers
Acquire a will of their own
And descend to her ankles.

He reads her a poem.

It is better
Than her best vibrator.

Their love affair
Begins.

They then discover
That a god of accidents,
Of comic misfortunes
Is meddling in their business.

Stronger than lust.
Much stronger than poetry.

This will end
Badly –
That is to say
With a diminuendo.

Cafard

I feel it rolling up
Like a sea-mist,
Covering the beach
Where I dream I am standing.

A strange dream,
In the midst of so many,
Whose faces are dim,
Whose voices are muffled.

There is a pale light
Now
As the mist swallows me,
Bilious and yellow.

My nostrils tickle.

I want to sneeze,
But cannot.

Changing Shape

Why does one say there must be more?
    When the time comes, then we must go.
    Whether the crossing's swift or slow,
A mist conceals the other shore.

I enter it: what happens then?
    Today I feel I must insist
    That I myself am more than mist,
Whatever's so with other men.

Why fill the future with my past?
    To be a vapour, and then less –
    A vacancy, a nothingness –
Would give my life a shape at last.

'Here for a Little While'

Here for a little while.
And then?
      Gone travelling.
The things I thought I knew
Dumbly unravelling.
My light becoming shade;
My calm a storm.
No truth in what was true –
My elements remade
Into a different form.

You hear all that and smile –
How can it be?
Most lives are on dry land;
Mine's now at sea.
There's thunder without sound;
My wake's an open wound,
Closing as this is said.

In Helsinki

The drunk woman
Clings to my arm.
No matter that I'm queer,
She wants to be soul-mates.

The words she'd like to say
Won't come out.
They're locked
In a dungeon in Babel.

Yet a moment ago
Something went
From me to her.

My poem flew
Straight to its target.

In the Henhouse

In the henhouse
They are all crouched down,
Hands under the hen's backside,
Waiting for the egg
She is going to lay.

'It's mine!'
Each of them thinks,
'It's got to be mine! –
The magic egg.
The egg that will make me rich!
After all, you can't divide it –
Just one egg –
And I'm the one who deserves it.
Surely the rest of them will see that,
Once I've my hand around it.'

And the hen thinks,
'This is ridiculous –
I feel like an old woman
With a choice of seven bedpans.
There's no dignity left
In this egg-laying business.
Given the chance
I'd pack it in
And go away.'

In Two Words

Surprised by the afflictions
That visited our parents,
Those inabilities
We once derided –
Seeing, hearing,
Walking, digesting –
We still refuse
To accept we are now
Exactly as they were.
In two words: past it.

Invitation to the Dance

'So you want to go to the ball?'
His father said.
And he said: 'Yes. Yes, I'll do it.'
Knowing what was being asked.

He dressed himself
In white tie and tails,
Hired of course,
And stood in the hallway waiting,
A young six-footer,
Handsome as the devil.

There was a footfall on the stairs,
A huge brocade skirt,
Powdered bosom,
Tiara and other jewels.

So he took his father's arm,
Led him to the limousine
Which was parked outside.

It wouldn't have occurred to him,
He said later,
To behave otherwise
With this distinguished older woman.

After that he knew
What he was,
Who he was,
Why he was.

Kosovo, 1999 – 1

What do the poets
Have to say about Kosovo?
Surely they can solve things
With a few phrases?
Where are their protests?
Their wise words?

Prince Lazar
Going down
Before the Turks;
Prince Lazar's bones
Travelling and returning
To Kosovo,
To holy Kosovo.

Yet this land is now
Inhabited by strangers –
What are they doing here?
They are building houses,
Breeding children,
Tilling the soil –
A soil which they tell us
Is holy to them too.

What do the poets
Have to say about Kosovo?

Kosovo, 1999 – 2

The news is
That there is no news
This morning.

There is a war somewhere,
But everyone agrees
The public must know
As little as possible
About it.

Nightscope pictures of distant explosions,
Close-ups of White House spokespersons,
References to genocide,
And, for balance,
Statements about 'unprovoked aggression'.

The television also
Shows sleek black limousines
In the middle distance.
One cannot pick out the faces
Through their darkened windows.

Left-Handed

How are you doing
Up there on Parnassus –
Donne, Marvell, Rochester, Raleigh –
You who wrote poems
With the left hand only?

When you come close
Blind Homer
Senses your presence.
He turns away
To talk to Milton,
Equally blind.

Do you feel uneasy
Among all these
Who made it a lifework?

You are not like them.
You look out idly
From your shining mountain
And see the world
With its rage and folly,
Tears and laughter.

Sometimes, but rarely,
That incorporeal
Impatient left hand
Finds itself longing
To seize a pen.

Leviathan

Dark caves where blind fish swim.
Great depths where dim lights burn,
And fierce Leviathan
Lies waiting for his return.

Oh see him rising up!
The water flees his sides.
Above him on the wind
One flashing seagull rides.

Now far away on land,
Deep in their hidden caves,
The fish begin to leap,
Responsive to those waves.

World moving to an end
With a resistless flow.
In daylight none of this –
In dreams we have it so.

'Lost Roads…'

'Lost roads, lost roads,' we say.
We cannot figure out
How was it that the way
Suddenly turned about
And brought us where we are.
Yet we should bless that star
Which led us so astray,
Because, if we had gone
Straight onward, as intended,
Our story would be one
Long ago lost, and ended.

Minotaur

It's no problem,
Finding your way
To where the minotaur
Lives in hiding.

One turn,
Then another –
You are there in no time,
Ready for combat.

It's not even
Difficult to kill him.
He cannot survive
Your sharpened gaze.

The trick is
To find a way back,
Step by step,
Through the sweaty darkness.

You pray:
'Thread do not break,'
But still it slips
From your numb fingers.

It's a bull's head now
Upon your shoulders.

My Mother

You clamoured so you couldn't hear yourself
Inside.
You cut short answers so as not to have to listen
To questions, inside.
You talked
Endlessly, endlessly,
Blocking doorways,
Monopolising meal-times
With the word 'I' –
And again 'I'.

Somewhere, long ago,
There was a child who lost her mother,
And then her father,
Who lived with cousins,
Much older,
Who didn't really want her,
Who went to boarding school
And wore black stockings
By a cold, grey sea.

Polio lamed you.
War took nearly all
The men you might have married.

With your big nose,
You never looked right
In flapper dresses.

I'm lucky to be here.

Why is There no Female Michelangelo?

(for Judy Chicago)

Who are they, these women
Painting frescos in churches,
Posing their female apprentices
Nude for male martyrdoms?
Who are these young girls
Portrayed with false beards
As St Joseph with the Christ Child?

They exist
In an alternative universe.

Imagine a world
Where they worship the Mother,
Not the Father,
The Daughter,
Not the Son.

Would there then be any need
For Crucifixions and Martyrdoms?
For an art about pain?

If there is no female Michelangelo
Maybe it is because
Humanity invented
The wrong kind of god.

Obituaries

Today
The obituaries are celebrating
Indomitable widows –
I will not leave one of those,
Nor chicks, children, heirs.
Just a large pile
Of inanimate objects,
Leftovers
From a life spent pursuing
One butterfly
And then another.
Who will pick over
My remains,
And does it matter?
No.
Let the widows go to their rest
Unmolested,
And me to mine.

Oh God, Oh God

Oh god, oh god,
Why does it have to be
Edged and saw-toothed?
It's not what I,
At my beginnings,
Set out to create:
Poems like a modern Bellini –
Vincenzo, Giovanni,
Or even that sweetish cocktail,
Dulcet to a fault.

Late in life I discovered
What I could do with a camera.
My boys embracing
Are full of romantic love.
Even if they don't feel it,
Love appears
When I pick the frame
And click.

Alas, this other art
I embraced so much earlier
Remains for me
A mouthful of thistles
Pre-masticated,
Just for you.

Poetry

The profoundly dysfunctional,
The professionally unhappy –
There's a fee I don't want to pay
To enter that particular Parnassus,
Though everyone who enters
Gets to be a genius.

Nor do I want to be captive
There in the quarry,
Bellowing my pain,
Hurling metaphors like boulders,
Using the sticks of dynamite they allow me
To blast great chunks
From the granite of language.

Better to be passing through,
And passed through.

I eat life,
And shit poetry.

Poetry Reading

The poets think
They want to be heard.

The poets
Don't want to listen.

How can any words
Be better than mine?

So I stand here
Alone on the platform
Spinning them out –
These words that are mine.
My own.
Me.

They harden around me
Like a wall of crystal.

Rain in Buenos Aires

The rain falls on this fragment of Europe
Which is so far from Europe.

It encloses the statues of generals
In cabinets of crystal
And washes the bird-shit
From coiffures of classical goddesses
While puddles in the gutters
Reflect an Indian sky.

They part the clouds,
The forgotten gods of the Indians,
And see the racing taxis,
Girls in high heels
Cursing the weather in Spanish.

What do they feel?
Do they feel anything
As they hold up this sky,
Keep the planets rolling across it?

Why take so much trouble
For people who do not know them?

They look down.
They see the tribes
Decked in their paint and feathers —
For the gods nothing has changed,
Nothing at all.

Riding the Drum

They call it
'Riding the drum' –
A drum itself painted
With records of journeys.

To the far north.
To the far south.
To caverns underground.
To the Pole Star.

What is the shaman doing?
Beating his drum,
Entering his trance,
He is trying to discover
Another self,
An escape from the self,
A way of becoming the other.

And what is this other?
A bird, a beast, a fish,
A being of the opposite gender.

He returns wearing feathers or scales.
He returns with his balls cut off.
He returns with aching shins,
A dry mouth,
The feeling that death has entered
And sits in the hollow of his bones
Urging yet one more journey.

Condemned to play
The villain's part:
Baba Yaga,
The bad witch
In a Russian fairytale.

Let me try to tell it
Quite differently.

Born a nomad,
Ignorant
Of the idea of home.
What did you want?
Most of all
To fit in somewhere.

Your love affairs
Were experimental fictions
To which you could never
Find the right ending.

The last of them
Was the tale of the strong man
With the mad wife.

You folded him in your nightgown.
When you woke next morning
You were three in a bed.

Russian Elegy – 2

A strolling player
With a gift for impersonating
Innocent princesses,
You caught the eye
Of someone
Who was not quite a prince.

Your two realms
Never meshed.
He could not understand
The sweaty faces
And simple jokes
After the performance.

What he wanted
Was Princess Aurora
Perpetually on tiptoe.

And you?
What you wanted
Was the one thing
He couldn't give you –
Love in your sense.

Perhaps in his culture
There was no word for it.

The Great Poet

All these women
Worship the cock
Of the great poet.

He owes them an orgasm.
Or several.

Tumescent in his jeans,
He is ready to oblige.

Of course they have not read
Many of his verses,
Which are about solitude –
The high, thin screech
Of the night owl's prey
Somewhere far off
In a darkened woodland.

The landscape in his head
Might make them fearful.
Why should they wish
To have it described?

The Stone Ship

(Åles Stenar, near Malmö)

The bright sky above,
The cows lowing
As they scratch themselves on the stones,
All say, 'Empty, empty.'
The sea below is metal
That does not resound.
There is an absence here
That needs to be explained.

Perhaps Tristan fled to the north,
And not to Britanny.
It was here that he laid his bones,
Far from Iseult.
This is his rib-cage,
Also the boat
In which he made his voyage,
Bleeding and stone-heavy
With the end of hope.

Words – 1

(in memoriam Alain Bosquet)

A poet dies. Or not. Words
He wrote resonate somewhere,
Birds of night take up his cries.
A dream visits a child. Far
Off a wave falls on a beach.
Somewhere a star silently
Falls, like a drop down a pane
Of glass. Linked together, these
Make the event we call death.
We could call it a new start.

Words – 2

There are things
Words want you to say
More than you want
To say them.

You turn them one way.
They writhe like snakes,
Twist on your tongue,
And strike.

You feel the poison
Thrill in your veins.

You spit it out.

It sets fire
To the ears and minds
Of others.

Afterword

This collection consists of poems drawn from four earlier books in commercial publication, the most recent of which was published in 1974. It also includes poems written in the quarter of a century since that date. Those readers who know my earlier collections will see that I have omitted most of the longer poems, notably the dramatic monologues associated with the 'Group', the poetry reading and discussion group I once chaired, which was for a time very influential. The reason for omitting them is that, while I think they are quite good of their sort, I also think they are not good enough, especially when they are compared with the work of Robert Browning, the master of this genre.

Changing Shape chronicles a slow technical evolution accompanied by a fairly radical personal one. The early poems are usually in strict forms, then come unrhymed poems in syllabics, then, more recently, poems in completely free forms. This progression is not consistent – there are rhymed poems among the later pieces, among them the title poem – but the main line of development is clear. What I have been looking for, in all this, is a kind of poetry which conveys as simply, rapidly and effectively as possible what I think and feel at the moment of writing. Writing poetry, for me, is also a process of finding out. Very often, I do not in fact know what the thought or emotion actually is until the poem in hand tells me.

The English tradition offers a place to two very different sorts of poets. There are those who are lifelong professionals – poetry is central to their existence. Chaucer, Milton, Dryden, Pope, Wordsworth, Tennyson and Browning come immediately to mind. Then there are many poets, including some important ones, and many more who are delightful but usually classified as minor, for whom poetry has always been a secondary activity. This group includes some of the poets I like best, such as Wyatt, Raleigh and Rochester. I don't think any one of these would have said that writing poems was the main aim of his existence. I would place myself within this category.

I started off with the idea that I might become a professional poet. Gradually, I discovered that that was not in fact what I wanted to do with my life. This was one of the reasons why, professionally, I gradually drifted out of the British poetry world and into the much larger one of international contemporary art. The art world has been good to me and I am grateful. I have travelled widely and experienced many different countries and societies as a result of my connection to it. I have also been in contact with aesthetic attitudes which would find little understanding or sympathy in the world of English literature. I do not sympathise with all of these, but I am glad to know about them. More recently, through my membership of the Académie Européenne de Poésie, I have been in touch with a number of very distinguished poets writing in a range of familiar and unfamiliar foreign languages. Their approach to the art of writing poetry is often substantially different from those which prevail in Britain or even in the USA.

There is no way of shutting out experiences of this sort if one wants to continue to write poetry, and I have never attempted to do so. Some things may come as a surprise even to people who are familiar with my work as an art historian and art critic. For example, there are some pieces here which refer to French poetry of the Middle Ages, and in particular to the Tristan legend. Obliquely, these stem from the fact that I once wrote a biography of Joan of Arc, which led me towards a fascination with the French medieval world in general.

My involvement with the story of Joan of Arc may suggest that I have a temperament which is essentially religious. This both is and is not the case. I would describe myself as being a reluctant sceptic, just as I am a reluctant sensualist and a reluctant homosexual. There are poems on all these themes in *Changing Shape*. The book is the fragmentary autobiography of someone who has never quite known what he wanted to be, while being, at the same time, often quite certain about what he wanted to do. In other words, it is a text about both deliberate and involuntary self-transformation. I hope there may still be some further transformations available to me in the future.